BUILDING MENTAL TOUGHNESS IN SPORT

AN INTRODUCTION INTO SPORTS PSYCHOLOGY FOR ATHLETES

"The last few inches of the body make the biggest difference in sport – yet are those most forget to train."

- Benjamin Bonetti

HOW TO CONNECT WITH OTHER AMAZING ATHLETES
Head to the website to connect with our other social channels, read the latest blogs, sign up for updates and apply for your coaching session!
HTTP://WWW.100NMAN.COM

First published in Great Britain for Benjamin Bonetti

Copyright © Benjamin Bonetti 2016

Benjamin Bonetti asserts the moral rights to be identified as the author of this work.

A catalogue record for this book is available from the British Library.

Find out more: info@100nman.com

All rights are reserved. No part of this publication may be reproduced, stored in a retrieval system or transmitted in any form or by any means, electronic, mechanical, photocopying, recording or otherwise, without prior permission in writing from Benjamin Bonetti.

This book is sold subject to the condition that it shall not, by way of trade or otherwise, be lent, resold, hired out, or otherwise circulated without the publisher's prior consent in any form of binding or cover other than that in which it is published and without a similar condition including this condition being imposed on the subsequent publisher.

This book is dedicated to the following:

You

CONTENTS

Introduction	15
Ownership Over Thoughts	25
Expectations	35
Revenge The Hidden Evil Living Within Us.	47
Challenges	57
Sticking To The Plan	61
Strategies For Conflict States	67
Removing Labels	71
Stop Settling The Second-Best	77
Knowing When To Focus	83
When Is It Time To Celebrate?	89
Referencing	95
Self-Sabotage	101
Truth	107
Perception And Lies	113
Overloading The Mind	119
Relationships	123
Forgiveness	129
Creating A High Demanding Attitude	135
My Scruffy Hair	141
The Desert Island	147
Person And Character	153
Are You Selfish?	159
What Is The Intention Of This Thought?	165
Nature Versus Nurture	171
Practice On Your Own.	177

FOREWORD

This introduction into increasing mental toughness is not designed to be the sole solution to *your search* for improvement but a thought provoking tool. It is a snippet of what's available in our more comprehensive coaching platforms or the *"The New Encyclopaedia of Sports Psychology"*.

No formats, just words: **Enjoy.**

WHO OWNS YOU?

🎯 Who are *you*?

___

🎯 What is *your* legacy?

___

🎯 How will *you* be remembered in 10 lifetimes to come?

INTRODUCTION

I'm here to help you understand the choices that you've made, the reasons *why* you're doing what you're doing and perhaps a number of questions that you've had that still remain unanswered.

I've been coaching people for the last 10 years and during that time, most of the questions I've had from clients are the same. The same questions come from business owners, entrepreneurs, parents, children and athletes. Everybody faces the same challenges, and it's because of one particular reason.

We haven't been taught how to *think*!

Think about it? When was the last time that you entered into a space where they taught *you* strategies that improved your ability to think?

Very likely NEVER.

So what are the questions and why are they always the same variations, despite the very different upbringings, beliefs and needs?

The questions asked are generally based on how *you* become better, how you can increase *your* confidence, how you can keep motivated when times are tough, where you're going wrong, why others don't understand *you* or even why you don't understand yourself.

You may also fear the unknown, fear failure and success. And ultimately, you believe you're not good enough.

WHY?

I'm going to help you manage those thoughts, manage yourself and a whole lot more…some *will* make sense to you and other things not so much…but in knowing them, you have an increased awareness in the choices you make – but more on this later.

Before we get started, you may want to grab a pen and a notebook. I suggest a notebook because then you have the ability to refer back to it and continue to build upon those thoughts and develop strategies that you can reflect on in the future.

An A5 type notebook works best. Use each new page as a *progression* in your life and have the ability to line out those documented aspects once completed – there are a few select choices on our website.

Within this, we are going to work through a systematic program that will offer you the journey of realisation and build upon a better version of self. There will be conflict, there will be the need to supply me with trust, and you will need to take action.

So to start with, it is important that we align ourselves not to the past but to the future version of self.

The major difference is that I'm making the assumption that you're here because the past version of self is not good enough. It can either be improved or offers little in terms of internal fulfilment.

The future version of self is perhaps a realisation that there is more to life, that there is more to you and that time is ticking, and it's important for you to achieve the percentage of what you intended, perhaps as a child.

Or you're being coached at the moment, and you're questioning the ability of that coach and whether it's a *true* reflection of your own growth and development, and you're just checking out whether I can offer any confirmation or clarity over those thoughts.

To control these thoughts, we first must understand that despite the mind being complex, the system actually is incredibly simple. And if you're in that place of frustration, you can give yourself permission now to *forgive*.

Forgive because you can't be expected to understand something that you've not been taught and if you're frustrated because you are stuck, the likelihood is that you're simply missing knowing where to go to access the next piece of the puzzle.

I'm making the assumption that at your school, college, university or even within a job, you weren't given direct or clear instructions on how your *thought* processes work and how to utilise them in the best possible way.

Because of this, I'm going invite you to forgive – I'm repeating this but it's essential. All the time that you're holding onto that past anger, frustration, resentment or living within a state of ego, you'll be locked into those limitations.

Forgive yourself *now* for not knowing – if you don't feel that it is time, and you like the immersion within that past pain, then I'm not sure that this really is the right time for you, and that is also okay.

I remember talking with a business owner who applied for coaching a few years ago that became increasingly frustrated when I told him that the world wasn't ready for his new thinking, and I couldn't work with that. Only to be told three years later when we met again that I was right. Two years after that, I saw an opening and called him – he is now on one of the most influential speaking circuits talking about timing.

You see – if you are not prepared to be truthful about your timing or ability, then you're miles behind of where you should be. You can only trick the mind/body energy for so long until the person's ability – overpowers the character that you've been playing.

Make sense? Great, let's move on.

So with your pen and notebook, I want you to write down quickly (within 3 minutes) without conscious effort what you want to change. And more importantly, *why* you want to change for the better. Specifics are essential at this stage, so I'd rather you complete just one thing and have all the specifics than a long list of stuff with no real detail.

STOP AND COMPLETE THIS NOW!

_____

_____

_____

_____

_____

_____

I ask this now because I've worked with hundreds of people over the last 10 years, and many have come through my door because they've been forced and they're not freely willing to make changes of their own accord.

Introduction

They've been told that they have an issue or a problem, perhaps even a bad habit and only seek help because it's in conflict with another ideal of the world and how they should be living it.

If you're not ready to change yet, then *stop* right here and avoid the temptation to waste your time because it won't work. This is applicable to all aspects of life, from relationships to those standing at a workbench for 10 hours per day, 5 days a week complaining about how unhappy they are and have been for the last 20 years.

The person who smokes that doesn't want to give up will always find a way to return to that bad habit. There are a few who break the mould but when you dig deep enough, they just conform to this thinking.

Until you reach the point where the future version of pain is strong *enough*, avoid the temptation to lie to yourself or lie to others because you'll find a way to get back into that old thinking pattern because it's comfortable.

Hopefully, this is a bit of a wake up to those who aren't convinced.

GIVE UP NOW!

If you're still here, then I believe that you are one of the select few, 17% of those who start wouldn't have completed the first exercise and about 4% would have turned off to any suggestion by now.

For those remaining, I believe that you're reading this because of something great;

I want you to truly know and honestly answer why now is the right time?

The second thing to consider is that you have limited control on the factors outside self, but have absolute control on how they are represented, so it's important to *understand* that you're just going to have to accept some things.

You don't have control over the weather, but you do have control over your diet - it's as simple as that.

[As you start to evolve your thinking into a new space, you'll notice the words that others use and how sometimes they become caught up in the dramas of the uncontrollable.]

You also have to be prepared to delete the aspects of your past and those around you in the present that aren't supporting the future version of self that you desire today.

You know already internally what changes you're going to have to make and there may be those that will become hurt in the process, but ultimately you're only hurting yourself and prolonging that pain by allowing it to continue (whatever it is).

HAS THIS TRIGGERED ANY CONNECTION?

Once you've decided on the level of commitment and how much you WANT to change, then we move on to knowing who you are, not the inherited belief about who you are but the truth about who you are right now, and then we build upon that to find your legacy, making the assumption that you don't know it already.

You see, the past is not a representation of who you are and neither is the future.

Consciously deciding on who you are in the present and how you're acting in the present moment will determine what you're going to achieve.

This is the secret to success.

Introduction

Because of the importance of understanding the difference between the past and the future version of self, I'd invite you *right now* to be accepting of change and be prepared to do what it takes when you face challenges.

Some of what I'm saying may not make sense to you right now, and that's okay because just by listening to the words, you are absorbing all you need to ensure that you're aligning yourself to the *true* and honest future version of self.

So let's get started.

ARE YOU DE-SERV-ING?

Benjamin Bonetti

OWNERSHIP OVER THOUGHTS

As we begin to change as humans, it is important to understand that we take ownership over thoughts because our thoughts become behaviours, which become either our enjoyment or our failures.

It begins with ownership – I'm not going to break down the chemical reactions of the brain or the various *connections* with the nervous system. I just want you to know that you're connected. That you've got to take *ownership*, and the sooner that you do, the sooner you'll be able to understand how to manipulate the thoughts alone to produce exactly what you want.

Manipulate until a positive habit is formed and no conscious consideration is made.

For years, we been told there's a difference between the mind and body, but in truth, for me, there is only one, and that is *self* – it combines all that we are and most importantly, all that we create.

If you've read any of my previous work, you *understand* that I talk about the three pillars of success, these being:

Nutrition: What you consume, passes your lips and allows for physical growth and development, repair and recovery. Supporting fitness and mindful well-being. This is usually the first thing that athletes consider changing when they meet a blockage, but in truth, it is usually the last thing they take seriously.

Fitness: What enables the body to mobilise more productively in a way that supports thoughts and behaviours. In a similar way to a high functioning machine, the greater the understanding of the mechanics, the more refined we are able to tune. This is usually the first thing to change and the main focus for continued growth and development.

Mindful Well-being: The clarity of the thoughts that supports nutrition and fitness. How clear you can think in the present moment and what allows further thinking and development. Despite being the last thing that athletes consider changing, in a recent study, 87% of athletes believed it was the biggest restriction they had.

An athlete cannot run with money in his pockets. He must run with hope in his heart and dreams in his head."
Emil Zatopek

Why is it divided into the three?

You see this version of self; the one that is reading this has the choice to be many different characters and is often confused as to which character they are to be playing. And if you *think* about it in your current life, the likelihood is that you'll be playing at least one or two right now.

You could be playing parents or partners, business owners or employees, athletes or coaches. And this is where most of the identity confusion takes place. I liken this to an actor who, when playing many characters onstage and under pressure, has the potential to mix up the lines, being confused over who says what and when they are supposed to deliver. The more characters you play, the greater the *increase* in those behaviours that are displayed that are considered to be 'out of character'.

The mind functions in a very similar way. So in order to create a better version of self, and one that supports you in the most *productive* and helpful way, you are to remove the clouded mist of these various characters and understand who you are.

47% of conflicts most commonly occur within athletes as they attempt to work out their identity – usually as a result of those who have pursued a sport as a result of external pressure. Living perhaps to the *inherited* beliefs passed on by parents, teachers, coaches or anyone else that has played a part within your growth and development so far.

If you are an athlete, I'm going to guess that you've been into some dark places based on the pressures, and the high *expectations* of those mentioned above – the good news is that there is little need for you to enter this space again.

Unless of course, you have taken ownership over this being the only person you can be.

So I want you to know as you *develop* and grow and you remove some of the characters, you will meet some conflict. I want you to be okay with that, be okay with growth and development, understanding that there will be a loss, which will make room to build upon the true version of self.

We replace, we do not remove.

One important factor: You need to *stop* wasting time.

You need to stop wasting time living someone else's dream. You need to think about what is important for you and why now is *the right time* for you to take the action needed to become that person. To live by your own standards, live by your own expectations and to be honest with yourself.

Because with every day that passes that you are not realising that dream, you are wasting time, wasting time that cannot be recouped, and wasting the time of those *investing* in you – harsh but true, and you know it deep down.

Time for a clear out, so answer the following questions:

🎯 Who are you?

_____

_____

_____

_____

_____

🎯 Why are you not taking action to live your life?

_____

_____

_____

_____

_____

🎯 What are you holding onto?

_____
_____
_____
_____
_____
_____

🎯 What happens if you fail to make the changes needed?

_____
_____
_____
_____
_____
_____
_____
_____
_____

🎯 Why is now the right time to change?

_____
_____
_____

🎯 Why should you take control over your life?

_____
_____
_____
_____
_____
_____

🎯 What inherited beliefs about self-do you have?

_____
_____
_____
_____
_____
_____

Ownership Over Thoughts

ARE YOU HAP-PY?

EXPECTATIONS

I welcome you to give up any ideas about what you think you can learn here and now, removing any *thoughts* that you've had before starting and remove any ideas about where perhaps it's going to lead you.

If another athlete has recommended this program, then remove the expectation – your *results* will be different.

The reason I invited to do this is because in society we've become like sheep, we've become people that follow instructions despite understanding and realising what *truth* is. Here and now I'm giving you the space to free yourself from these shackles, and take ownership of your life, your athletic performance and open up the possibility to being more than you are being told.

This isn't some alternative style thinking like some cynical people would suggest, THIS IS REAL. Many of the people that come into my clinic or coaching practise believe that they are broken, broken as a result of the comparison they are making to an image not even created by their own thoughts. They are not to blame nor is there anything wrong. They are not ill, broken or require fixing – like nearly all *assume*.

Our mind is a sponge, it draws in what we guide it to and on some occasions, we dip it in the wrong bucket. Not only that, but it has to contend with the masses of 'sales' and manipulation messages on a daily basis.

And we only have to look at food labels to understand this further, with many people *accepting* that a ready-made meal is healthier than fresh whole fruits and vegetables. We know what the *truth* is but sometimes the lazy part of thinking accepts what we're being told and doesn't question the answers we're being given.

[Behind almost every large branded item is a team of marketers headed by some of the world's leading psychologists – it's hard to escape unless you shift thinking into a questioning mindset]

How do we get over this?

We need to relearn how to *think*, relearn how to question what would be sold, and retrain that lazy habit to become part of that better version of self. Never has my son come home from school and explained to me how he spent the day learning how to improve his thoughts to produce better results through asking better questions, nor do his peers walk around the supermarket questioning the labels on truth – like he's been taught.

> *Persistence can change failure into extraordinary achievement.*
> **Marv Levy**

Rather, he is being given information to regurgitate.

I'm inviting you to *change* that way of thinking, to forge a new dynamic version of self that is stimulated by regaining control over your thoughts and the questions you are asking, and as a result, your behaviour.

This may take some time, and I'm okay with that as you enter into a self-revolution, not evolution.

But most of it will be based on an external reflection of self and as a result of that and the misalignment, many athletes fail. They enter a downward spiral of *accepting* a fake truth (to which they have been sold) and in which they have reached disappointment, and then they give up.

This is not truth. Truth is only based on the present, in me talking and in you reading, digesting the information I'm relaying to you, going to the past to make sense of it all and then coming back to the present to produce a connection.

This is truth – for now.

The major advancements I've made within the sports community and with an athlete isn't regurgitating age old concepts or theories but using the tens of thousands of hours working with the elite to understand what works – what is *proven* to deliver – then apply those models to new simplified strategies.

Take a moment to think about this expanded notion:

The past is gone; hence it's called the past. The future is yet to happen. And you have control over neither. Sure you can act now, stop reading or listening, hit the pause button, then make a cup of tea and come back, but each of those individual sections will be based on the *present* moment, none of which you have the ability to return to and none of which you will have the ability to change.

So I'm inviting you to relinquish those old ways of thinking, live in a harsh reality that ONLY YOU have *control* in the present and to not bother exercising any energy in either the past or the future.

Now as a result of thinking in this new way, you will encounter not only new thinking patterns but also plenty of resistance.

And this is fine and simply highlights that you're becoming more effective in questioning.

You will meet those who will prefer the old you, you'll be called selfish and even think at times that the past offered a better understanding of life and return to new habits. This is a humanist instinct to return to the *known*. This is the second habit you'll have to break.

On the topic of removing bad habits or thoughts, I want you to start thinking about the *choices* that you have and whether to reject or accept aspects of the external world. Perhaps even notice this from this point forward how willing others are to give their opinions about who you are, what you are to become and the reasons why.

The more you start to practice this, the more aware you will become about the external influences that have been building the foundations of your life, and how *accepting* you perhaps have been up until this moment.

Your eyes will start to open as a result, and you'll be more conscious over the company you keep and what you choose to *accept* or decline. From this, your perception of truth and reality will change because the projection of another is not the reflection of you or the reflection of them.

It is an attempt for them to connect and make sense of you and your behaviours.

Okay, so you've now removed another's impression of where you should live and where your boundaries are. I want you to ask yourself whether the thoughts and questions you're asking yourself are *supporting* you or supporting those old patterns.

Are you acting in the past, are you *thinking* in the past, are you utilising the past experiences to determine how your future my look, EVEN the way that you act?

PAUSE FOR A MOMENT TO DIGEST THIS!

The more that we live in the past, the more we produce the same results of what the past produced, and although that may be okay for some, I'm making the assumption here that you've moved beyond that way of thinking, and *now* it's time for you to truly live the way that you want.

Perhaps even the vision that you had as a child, the dreams and aspirations that you had during your younger days that are yet to materialise – perhaps you've known something that you've avoided until now and just with hearing it – *deciding* how things can't continue and why now is the right time.

Perhaps the only thing that has been holding you back in high performance is for you to take *control* over your life.

Here is a quick exercise for you.

> 🎯 Think back to when you were seven years old looking to the future. What did your future look like and what choices were you making at the time? Sure, the visions of a seven-year-old, for most anyway, are unlikely to draw a true representation of the future, but what if you were able to go back to that time and talk to that version of you – what would you say about the choices that you'd make?
>
> _____
>
> _____
>
> _____
>
> _____

🎯 In doing this simple exercise, you'll highlight perhaps those areas that weren't addressed or highlighted during the previous exercises. If needed, write them down now and think about why these have been brought up at the moment.

_____
_____
_____
_____
_____

🎯 What if now you looked at the future version of self, reflect back to your legacy statement, for the answers to the choices that you're making in the present moment?

What if you shifted this way of thinking? What would happen if you took the future as a representation of the choices that you made right now, and how would those choices be different?

_____
_____
_____
_____

> 🎯 Think about one choice you have to make today and note the differences in answers produced if you went to the future and acted, compared to the past and acted.
>
> Write them down now.
>
> _____
>
> _____
>
> _____
>
> _____
>
> _____
>
> _____

Now there are many theories about the hierarchy of needs, and I'm sure that you've come across several in any previous research that you've done. What I am going to ask you to do now is *trust* your gut.

Trust your gut knowing that it is *protecting* you from the dangers of life and SLOW DOWN – more on this later.

From experience, athletes tend to speed up every aspect of their life. They speed up the need in relationships, they speed up the need when it comes to *decisions* they make, and we also speed up the need to communicate, especially when restricted by time.

A recommendation here is to slow down. Pause before making choices.

Slow down, pause, think about your *future* self and act in the present.

If you are unsure how to do this, go to the website and download a copy of the meditation audio. Five minutes out first thing in the morning and then repeated in the evening has proven time and time again to stabilise thoughts and the ability to *think* with increased clarity.

Remember your internal processor limits you – the more you overload it, the more filtering it has to contend with.

ARE YOU SATISFIED?

REVENGE THE HIDDEN EVIL LIVING WITHIN US

I want to make this clear, revenge has never produced anything that will significantly *improve* your life for the better, unless of course, it is to prove someone wrong and waste masses of energy following the wrong path.

I meet many athletes years into their training who are looking to prove something, not because of an inner desire to better themselves but to prove something to someone who no longer matters – and even if they do, it is time to face the *reality* that it will never produce true fulfilment.

I'm sure this is something everyone has experienced at least once in their life, where the choice to follow a certain path was not based on an aspiration to *achieve* something for themselves it but was fuelled by the element of demonstration of strength.

I call this the inner idiot – we all have one that pops up every now and then.

The truth is, the only truth is your truth. The truth that you're living right now may not be in perfect alignment to your future self, so you're acting in the space of not truth – repetitive yes but it is essential that you bring *truth* into your thoughts, again challenging the characters that you've been playing out and establishing a person that is in control.

When you flip this way of thinking, some will call it selfish, but I want you to realise that when you're acting in the best interest of self, you no longer become selfish, but it becomes self-preservation. An active internal truth, internal *alignment* which many don't get.

Of course, there are those that believe that they're acting in truth and still selfish but only do so because they are misaligned – they are wolves. Conditionally taking but not for their own purpose or security, just because they can.

An odd statement I know, but from experience, when you really start to open your eyes, look for what is needed, *commit* 100% towards finding it without distraction, the solution will be there – you become the shepherd, no longer guided by social conformity or the expectations of another value or belief and no longer taking for the sake of it.

As you start to uncover the truth and flip this way of thinking, you'll notice more *opportunities* that support that future version of self – it has happened with every client I've ever worked with. The more they establish what they want, the more they SEE what is required to get themselves to that place. It's like the switch has finally been turned on and they are no longer living in darkness.

Just reflecting back to others from the moment, the opinion of others really doesn't count unless you choose to *accept* them. Thinking back to the attempt to prove others wrong, is there any aspect of your thinking that needs to be changed right now?

Because any misalignment will cause conflict, and it is usually in the times of *specific* need where this conflict will rear its ugly head. The objective is to remove any stresses, triggers of the past to ensure that when pressure is applied the state remains stable.

It's essential that you find your driving force, the thing that wakes you in the night, and the one key aspect that makes you unique and drives you to be the best. With all that I said about another's representation of how you should be living life, and with ownership, now it's important to *understand* that with this control comes its own challenges.

If you've been a passenger in your own life and are now taking the seat of the driver, you will encounter *new* challenges. You may have to make some stops along the way, and maybe a few detours; having control has its own responsibilities.

It's worth noting at this stage that there is going to be many backseat drivers, not just externally but internally too. And it's usually the internal backseat driver that will ask you to make unscheduled stops along the way.

To just be aware of this, living like there's no wrong, living in the present control of your destiny and seeking no approval from another based on their own standards representations of the world.

Which merges nicely onto judgement…

Judgement is a factor and an aspect that comes up with almost every client and there is no fault for this. We have created a society who judge based on materialistic possessions, a 'gold medal hierarchy,' which is very much external.

I'm going to invite you now to remove any judgement that you may have towards another and to love equality just for a few days to see how this vision of the world changes, perhaps even look to see what *fulfilment* means to you and where this vision may take you.

Do you look on to someone achieving what you previously wanted with anger, frustration or envy or look on with questions about their strategy?

Same mind – different thinking.

As you do, notice how the fight, flight or freeze response changes. How does the future version of self THINK when you encounter those challenges, and what is triggered *emotionally* that instigates the fight, flights or freeze response?

If it produces negative connections – even now, then FLIP IT. See how each of those challenges can be approached differently. See how when we remove judgement, we remove limitations of self and we align self to a legacy statement and act in the present moment.

> **Make sure your worst enemy doesn't live between your own two ears.**
> **Laird Hamilton**

In doing this, there is little room or need to fight, flight or freeze.

Because when you're unsure what to do, the autopilot kicks in and realigns you to that legacy statement. You only become lost when there is no destination set, and you've not mapped accordingly.

This demonstrates the importance of alignment.

There will be times when it goes to pot, and you can be okay with this. Because sometimes you have limited control, sometimes things won't go to plan, not because of anything that you've done, or there's been a lack of preparation, but because of certain factors that can't be controlled.

The importance is not what's gone wrong but how you can make it right. How you can move on *learning* if required and developing with the additional knowledge that this time provided?

YOU ARE CONNECTED WITHOUT KNOWING HOW

How you connect the dots is as a result of your internal belief and your representation of this meaning. It is said that 55% of the way we communicate is via physiology. Taking this further, this 55% is controlled *100%* by the language that we're using internally.

If the language is not aligned clearly, *focused* towards a future version of self, the behaviours demonstrated physically will not be supported.

AND

There will be times where others will try and hijack your thoughts. When they do, thank them internally for their contribution, make the choice to move on, only in a way that *supports* growth in the future vision.

As a result of this, what you'll find is that the impulsiveness of those negative thoughts will dissolve, and you'll be able to move on quickly into space in realignment.

I know it seems that I'm going on about truth, realignment, and future versions – but any athlete wanting to realise their full potential needs to adopt a forward-thinking *attitude* rather than one that pulls them back.

> 🎯 So quickly now, in just a few words, what does that future version of self look like? Perhaps just in five words, how would you quickly describe it to complete stranger?
>
> _____
>
> _____

The reinvention of self can be an exciting time, especially if you've been living another's dream without true ownership. Building and regaining control, and having ownership over your own life, will offer an increased level of focus and the determination and *mental toughness* unparalleled compared to those living in a mantra-focused state.

So control…

Control is having ownership over thoughts, seeing the intention behind the thoughts and understanding where those thoughts are trying to lead you.

So what I'm going to invite you to do is to question the intention of each of the thoughts that you have, and ask yourself where they're attempting to take you and then decide if it's where *you* want to go.

The purpose behind this strategy is obvious and will take a little conscious effort on your behalf until this habit is forged. Be aware of the past thought strategies that will attempt to creep back in, ensure that you create enough leverage to ensure that is not an option for you and it's certainly not your choice to be mediocre or *accept* second place.

Answer this:

🎯 What thoughts are you dominated by and why?

_____

_____

_____

_____

I mentioned this before but I think it's important to reconfirm. I don't believe in mantras, and the reason I don't believe in mantras is because they are generally someone else's, and even when you create your own, they are only truth and relevant based on when they were created.

So I'm going to invite you to remove them, and if you feel the need that you can't live without them, look to create a mantra based on the *present* moment exactly when you need it.

Therefore just be.

ARE YOU COMMITED?

CHALLENGES

I think it's important to reiterate the need to remove yourself from the dramas of another's life. Sure, there are those people that enjoy the pain and suffering and the traumas of the world. Before you own your journey to *high performance,* it's essential that you live in a space that is only supportive. You could call it a bubble, but I prefer to call it an energy focused attitude.

Think for a moment why you would waste a moment of your life to support an unhealthy or unproductive thinking pattern. You may have already been down this path when you outlined forgiveness but spend just a moment *thinking* about why perhaps you've been attracted to those or those places in the past.

🎯 Perhaps, this is why now would be a good time to make the break and how you can identify quickly those times where the drama is being shown and your strategy for the removal.

_____

_____

_____

_____

ARE YOU SURE ?

STICKING TO THE PLAN

I've been known to ask my clients to remove themselves from everything that doesn't positively support the plan. I have found that having a no matter what *attitude* allows athletes to quickly within the present moment decide whether to immerse themselves or move on. Similar to what we just mentioned.

I have already mentioned the importance of being aware of the backseat driver attempting to override your path and prompt change for their own best interests.

So begin to *question* everything – this isn't to enter a cynical state but to own all that you see and accept.

And by doing so, you remove the variables outside of your control, and as a result, have the ability to fine tune your strategy until you reach that point that perfectly *supports* you in the most dynamic way.

Once you've fine-tuned, you can then opt to open up self to those dramas, however, from experience, most will distance them further and further *attract* those who support their current mindset.

🎯 Tell me your plan for the next 24hrs:

_____
_____
_____
_____
_____

🎯 Tell me your plan for the next 3 days:

_____
_____
_____
_____
_____

🎯 Tell me your plan for the next 7 days:

_____
_____
_____

Sticking To The Plan

🎯 Tell me your plan for the next 6 months:

_____

_____

_____

_____

_____

_____

🎯 Tell me your plan for the next 12 months:

_____

_____

_____

_____

_____

ARE YOU BROKEN?

STRATEGIES FOR CONFLICT STATES

This is something that you can easily adopt, as said previously, you could either immerse yourself in the dramas of life or move on quickly to something that supports you.

By creating a strategy you can adopt when you identify yourself being partly or dragged into that environment that is unsupportive to *overall* well-being.

For some it simply means to walk away, while for others, it can be a simple yes or no. Remember to have ownership over choice, the choice to either continue or to remove yourself.

What I am not saying is that you should walk away from anyone that says anything negative, but to spend your time wisely. Hours spent scanning social media at the dramas of people you don't even know is unlikely to have any *positive* impact when this time could be spent researching an optimised nutrition plan or increasing slow movement techniques.

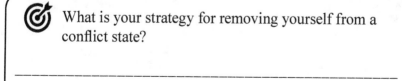

What is your strategy for removing yourself from a conflict state?

_____

_____

ARE YOU THE AN-SWER?

REMOVING LABELS

The quicker you are able to remove the labels of the past, the sooner you'll be able to realise the true *deserving* of self without limitations. I have been guilty of this in the past living within the boundaries inherited from others and their limitations of the 'possible'.

I had a fortunate upbringing, but even despite this, there are still limitations and expectations to *prove*. To me, the more labels you're able to remove, the further you can go to seek those opportunities.

We all know the rags to riches stories, the one in a million chance to break free, and the lottery winners of the world. But what about us every day folk, those who go against the odds on a daily basis and for some like me, don't place our *faith* in the lottery?

Just think about it for moment. What if the answers to all of your challenges were slightly outside of the limitations that you've inherited? Wouldn't it be wise to go to that place to *expand* your field of play, so that you can have your option to either accept or decline what those new boundaries offer.

For me, I found more suited opportunities at the far reaches of my limitations than those in the places where I thought I belonged. Therefore, I'm going to invite you right now to check these places out, to *explore* the limitations beyond where you've been told you should be and see what you can find.

You have nothing to lose but plenty to gain – even in removing that sense of belonging.

And then when we think about it, for most it is the parents that add this belonging, and even with this being said, it's important that we understand that for most parents they did their best. As a parent myself, I want the best and act in a way that supports this, as we're *unique*. We want the best for them and their intentions may not be what is suited for us.

> **❝ Champions keep playing until they get it right.**
> **Billie Jean King**

Avoid the temptation to seek praise, or approval but live in alignment. When I reached this place of internal *belief* – one that I'd created for myself and not one I'd chosen to accept – my life changed.

You can be emotional when needed, and that's fine but just know that the quicker that you regain control thoughts, the sooner you're able to realise the direction forward. I've had clients spend two days in the 'down state of reflection' only to come out stronger once they've decided to PULL THEMSELVES together and stop wasting time.

Because fighting the inner war has never proven to amount to anything worth living. It's important to be *truthful* here; why could now be the right time to forgive the past and live in the now?

> 🎯 What limitations have you accepted from another?
> _____
> _____

🎯 Why would now be a good time to release yourself from these?

___

___

___

___

___

🎯 What new beliefs can you accept and why?

___

___

___

___

___

___

___

___

ARE YOU SUP- PORT- ED?

STOP SETTLING FOR SECOND-BEST

All too often, athletes are quite happy to be the number two, to take second-hand advice and not to *invest* in the best possible advice for them. To hire the mediocre coach, to settle for less than standard conditions and to become accustomed to being the person that they are.

Sure, any athlete starting out can't expect to have the best of everything, but you can certainly have the best of what is within reach; you can alter where you find the true *value*, something we've already covered.

If you think you deserve the best, you will find the best. If you think you deserve second-place, that's what you'll find also.

I was recently coaching a commonwealth athlete that failed to recognise this until highlighted. She'd reached a high level off the bat without any 'coaching' per se, completely alone and without any 'professional' involvement.

After creating a plan to incorporate coaching, her times reduced by 3% within just a few weeks.

Timing had a large part to play here, but for the most part, she had settled for 'not' coaching due to the fact that she didn't feel deserving.

Now, we all aren't as fortunate to reach this competitive level without coaching, but what can be learnt here is that the gains of having the best will significantly improve performance levels – FACT!

A note here: there are still some antiquated coaches in the world teaching 1940's training methods. Just as technology has advanced, sports *performance* has equally evolved – those who are stuck here will understand what I mean. Ensure that all members of your team are advancing with modern measuring techniques and are able to access the resources required to fine-tune your performance.

> **❝**
> *I became a good pitcher when I stopped trying to make them miss the ball and started trying to make them hit it.*
> **Sandy Koufax**

The car analogy would be; a Ferrari owner could take his car to a mechanic, the mechanic has a suitable understanding of the workings of an engine but doesn't specialise in high-performance engines; a tuning session will not be as productive as if he were to invest the 'difference' in a technician with the suitable equipment and understanding.

Just a note on difference – I'm one of the most expensive mindful coaches available when you look at the bottom figure – but the difference between the average and the high end is actually marginal. The reason I mention this is because when exploring coaches – make the choice not on price (as most do) but on the *difference*.

The difference at this end may be significantly less overall compared to someone who insists on a long drawn out coaching platform.

> 🎯 What are you accepting right now that requires change?
>
> _____
> _____
> _____
> _____
> _____
> _____
> _____
> _____
> _____
> _____
> _____
> _____
> _____
> _____
> _____
> _____
> _____
> _____

DO YOU HAVE CHO- ICE?

KNOWING WHEN TO FOCUS ON THE SMALLER POINTS

This is something that many people become mixed up in, and you may have already gone past this point. In this world we need both, we need those who *think* about the nuts and bolts, and we need those innovators who think in a space where the finer points don't matter.

Both have a place, but all too often, people live in those spaces and remain there. What I'm going to invite you to do is explore both.

Generalising below (not truth):

- An aircraft mechanic would be considered as nuts and bolts.
- An artist would be considered as the bigger picture.

For a short time, I'm going to invite you to live in the nuts and bolts when strategizing, and *look* at the bigger picture for the rest of the time. Doing so allows flexibility where it counts.

The more you develop and increase your confidence, the more you will rely on the future version of self for the solutions to present moment challenges, rather than looking to the past for the *answers*.

It's not about shelving the past issues and concerns but rather about dealing with them and accepting that a lot of effort can be wasted in reflecting on the past when the same amount of energy can be utilised in *the best way* to move forward and build a productive version of self.

When working with a client, it's only the first couple of sessions that we look to the past to resolve any issues, before making any forgiveness and then moving onto building solid foundations to act in the present.

Because who cares. Any person that should care is YOU. Allow others to judge, but that is their *truth*, there's no reason why you should have any kind of ownership over that – unless you freely accept.

So who cares? Only you and your best interests, and if it doesn't support it, then why hold onto it?

Let it go!!!

> 🎯 Why would now be a good time to release the judgment another has on you?
>
> _____
>
> _____
>
> _____
>
> _____
>
> _____

Another hard-hitting approach towards improvement and development is when you are facing an obstacle when you face challenges outside of your control, perhaps even lose the motivation.

This will happen, it's part of operating at that high-level that allows the lack of motivation to happen. Someone who is not competing at this high-level lacks the motivation and has little need to lack something that's not required.

Blah, blah, blah – and move on.

I said blah, blah, blah because it's often the people with all the excuses in the world who are the *reasons* why they're not moving.

In my world just get on with it.

That energy spent talking about all of the reasons why you can't should be used to find a way that you can. It's really as simple as that.

As I've said in the past, the removal of distractions is essential whether internal or external, and *the more that you commit* and align yourself with being that person, and the clearer the image, the quicker you will be able to release any negative distractions.

> 🎯 How can you interrupt these patterns in the future should they occur?
>
> _____
>
> _____
>
> _____
>
> _____
>
> _____

ARE YOU TAK-ING ACT-ION?

WHEN IS IT TIME TO CELEBRATE?

Once you've achieved the goal, you deserved it. There are plenty of concepts in the world that you should make and reward yourself with small rewards that continue to motivate you to the *higher* purpose?

And although I agree with it to a certain degree, very rarely do I meet someone who has rewarded themselves at the right time. Often it comes too early and as a result of limited *intention*. To me, celebration comes after the event, during reflection and at a time where that springboard goal is completed.

As I said all along, if you're happy being mediocre and living in that space, then that's fine by me. If you're looking for high performance, ready to take steps to be *higher* than self – then there is a little time to be celebrating anything other than completion.

It's a hard attitude to take, I have taken criticism for it – but I wouldn't reward my children for half tidying their room. The reward comes in the finish.

🎯 When would be an acceptable time for you to celebrate and why?

Time To Celebrate

HAVE YOU FORGIVEEN?

REFERENCING

Understanding where you currently go to find information is similar to how a library works. We have our own bank, filled and sorted in a way that your *internal* processor can quickly access so that certain actions can happen without a momentary pause.

Systematically filed and usually ordered in a way that is unique to you. With this being said, just as books can be misfiled, your internal library can also do so at times with time spent reorganising and adjusting to your new *mindset*.

In my library at home (the physical not mental) I order my books by topic/interest, not by the conventional author or book name. This way, should I ever need to reference a book based on a type of flower, I can chunk up from flowers to gardening, to nature and usually find the book title that suits the *solutions* or answer I'm looking for.

I file my mental library in a similar way, with the aisles for the larger topic, and the shelves with the genre and then the second subdivided to the specific topics. I utilise this system to work both ways. For example, if I were looking for a new set for swimming technique, I could either go directly to swimming and find the *solution* or to the fitness area and chunk down.

With most athletes; due to the high level of growth usually encountered, not much thought has been given to the organisation of their thoughts or all the *conscious* effort required to design a filing system whereby they can access these at any time.

They may seem like a processor is naturally taken care of by the subconscious mind, but the more control you take over how you file information internally, the more *control* you take over the speed at which you can access information. This technique has proven with clients to increase not only their mental endurance but also their memory.

Sure, aspects of life can be automated, such as breathing and various hierarchies of needs but for the most part, a conscious effort is given.

Think for a moment about how you file your information.

🎯 How could it be improved?

_____

_____

_____

_____

_____

🎯 How will the conscious act of filing the information bring about an increased awareness over what thoughts have been left to run their own course without any control over the use or need?

_____

_____

THINK FOR A MOMENT

If you encounter any difficulties in accessing this place, then spend a moment to meditate. Clear your mind of all thoughts, allow any thoughts to drift away and *visualise* a physical library, creating your own internal library based on this blueprint. See all that you need to see, and build in a way that allows you to regain control over what is placed on this internal aspect of self.

Remember a solution-focused-attitude when building this new filing system for your mind, and how perhaps the past could have anchored you to think in a certain way.

Taking ownership over how it can appear and how easily you can access the information you need is *understanding* the difference between the stuff you need and the stuff you want, and the difference it makes to the person you want to be and become.

When you shift your thinking and thoughts, you notice the energy *shift* and the conversations change, and as you do this, ask the question 'where can I go with this'?

Spend a moment to meditate in this place feeling comfortable and enjoy where it leads you.

WHO CON- TRO- LS YOU?

Benjamin Bonetti

SELF SABOTAGE

There is no doubt that every athlete would have experienced this at least once in their career, and I think it's something that almost every person, irrelevant of birthplace will encounter. It's rooted deep in one's energy and for humans, it's something that unless controlled or you are *aware* of it, can cause major disruptions or intermittent limitations.

Self-sabotage is usually encountered in one of two situations.

The first situation is where you've achieved an intended goal, and the drive and determination are lost shortly afterwards, thinking back to the springboard goal strategy, this avoids that moment of reduced productivity state.

The second and most common is where the athlete will sabotage shortly prior to the completion of the event. Because of the fear of the unknown post event and an *internal* need to draw out the completion.

Not spending too much time on this topic, if you established a quality legacy statement and adopted the springboard goal setting strategy, you'll avoid this self-sabotage altogether.

Highlighting this factor should have created awareness, perhaps even opened up that honest conversation internally. Ensure that this is something you avoid in the future by creating an awareness and strategy to adopt this self-sabotage creeping in.

Remember, it is the journey to high performance that produces the fulfilment. The medal or title is only valued for that micro-moment. Make the *legacy* the life and the medal or title, the by-product of living a life of purpose and value to self.

> 🎯 Where in the past have you sabotaged an event?

🎯 What can you do in the future to ensure that this strategy is broken?

_____
_____
_____
_____
_____
_____
_____
_____
_____
_____
_____
_____
_____
_____
_____
_____
_____

ACTING IN THE PRESENT?

TRUTH

I talk a lot about the need for truth and the importance of acting in a way that is *truthful* to self, and I do this because I meet so many people who on a daily basis are living the lies.

They are living in space that isn't supportive of who they want to be, caught up in the rat race of life, working in environments only to support the CEOs of that business, unhappy and unfulfilled – signed up to a debt culture.

The athletes on their journey to achieve high levels of performance and *betterment* must unsubscribe to this way of living. And at times being truthful can hurt, it can hurt others who have been caught up in the lies and internal deceit.

But after the forgiveness stage, and once you're able to subscribe yourself to the truth, there is no other way. For me, it's always been as simple as that: if you don't like it, then change it.

If you are waking up in the morning excited about going to the gym, following your *dreams* and aspirations, you have to cut back on certain luxuries in which you've been accustomed. Then what trumps what? What value have you placed over internal fulfilment?

This is only something that you can answer.

🎯 What truth needs to be realised right now?

_____
_____
_____
_____
_____
_____

🎯 Why have you avoided it in the past?

_____
_____
_____
_____
_____
_____
_____
_____
_____

🎯 Why is now the right time to make some changes to this past way of living?

IN LOVE WITH WHAT?

PERCEPTION AND LIES

This is one that takes a little while to get your head around especially if the previous exercise of becoming truthful with yourself has *highlighted* aspects of your life that perhaps you've been hiding from.

Perception and lies highlights where we fit truthfully into the equation.

For most athletes, the margins are either 20% over or 20% under the truth. Being either 20% better or worse of the actual figure. Now, these boundaries aren't necessarily so important, less so than people would naturally assume. For me, they highlight one fundamental factor – *purpose*.

- When someone over exaggerates the performance level, they do so because of the reason.

- When someone under-exaggerates the performance level, they do so because of a completely different reason to when they over exaggerate

In just saying this, it may have triggered an internal conversation with self and something you can *relate* to.

🎯 Why do you over exaggerate or under exaggerate?

🎯 Why would it be helpful for *you* to change?

🎯 How does acting in this truthful state bring about less conflict internally?

BEING TRUE?

OVERLOADING THE MIND

It's time to pause – there has been lots of information to consider, at times in just reading or listening, some of the content here may have challenged the way that you *believe*. You may be having doubts about your ability to achieve, whether to continue or whether to give up.

So now it's time to pause for a moment – be truthful with self, understand why *you* want this journey – and whether your legacy statement represents the true version you want to become.

And it's fine if it isn't. This is the time where you should make alterations to the statement and *align yourself* perfectly right now.

🎯 What is your legacy statement?

_____

_____

_____

_____

_____

VALUE VS. VALUES?

RELATIONSHIPS

You may think it's odd to talk about relationships in a book focused on improving an athlete's ability, but for me, the relationship you have with *self* has a bond greater than anything that can be produced through external coaching.

The way you communicate with yourself both in and out of sporting events will improve any *connection* you have, far greater than any nutritional or physical shifts you may encounter.

A relationship, when broken down, can be summarised in the word, relationship.

- How you relate.
- And the vessel in which you do 'ship'.

Relationships in modern society have taken its form into more of a partnership, a connection between two people, and of course this is true, but the relationship for me is more about the way in which you communicate and how it's done so.

The foundations of improving that relationship starts with the improvement in communication.

Think about:

- The words you use to describe yourself.
- The structure of the sentences used and how dramatically

the answers depend on the way that it's structured.
- And even those communications that you choose to remove yourself from as a result of the emotional drama created by subscribing.

Relationships, therefore, are the stepping stones that should be considered *right now*.

Here's a simple exercise to open up your awareness. Over the next two days, when communicating with others, *listen* to the words that they use.

When I say listen, I mean really listen. Understand how each word used is reflecting a conversation happening internally for them. How their projection is playing out *their* values and beliefs around their truth.

As you do this, digest what they are saying and how perhaps that past version of you would have taken this as truth and how perhaps it would've *affected* your internal relationship.

This is a brilliant exercise to use at work and even at home, and you'll find that the more you really listen to another person's way of communicating, the more you'll cautiously construct the conversations that you have internally and *be aware* of the words and the impact that all the questions have within your life.

> 🎯 Think about one person right now. How has their communication affected your thoughts in the past?
>
> _____
> _____
> _____
> _____

Relationships

ARE YOU LIS- TEN- ING?

FORGIVENESS

Again a topic that's been covered but it's important just to revisit, perhaps as your *mindset* has shifted and your understanding of other factors are now evolved.

If you find yourself still carrying any baggage of the past, any burdens or inherited beliefs, now is the time to perhaps revisit that aspect of the past and *forgive* all that is required in order for you to move forward with the freedom.

Forgiveness can be a simple phone conversation, can be a text message and can even become a message that isn't delivered to either self or another. It can be a message that is written down and burnt or an email that has been created and then deleted.

The intention of this is not to revisit the pain of the past but for it to dissolve and no longer become part of your strategies or your reflection.

The essential part here is to forgive the past to avoid any procrastination, get on and do and move on with the peace of mind that there is no future *need* to go to that space again.

And why would you? Why would you carry around with you any burden that does not positively support a *future* version of self. Why would you carry the inherited beliefs of another based on their own limitations? Why wouldn't you just forgive and move on?

🎯 Who do you need to forgive and why?

_____
_____
_____
_____
_____
_____
_____

🎯 What will happen if you continue to hold onto that baggage?

_____
_____
_____
_____
_____
_____
_____

🎯 What has been the purpose of holding onto that baggage for so long?

WHY BOT- ER?

CREATING A HIGH DEMANDING ATTITUDE

Living in this demanding space of growth and development almost will certainly bring around *mindful* fatigue, therefore within the schedule you've created already, I'd like you to revisit that place in time for at least 15 minutes of mindful meditation.

Although this is not an excessive amount of time, these few minutes spent consciously will often bring about increased clarity for the day and a more *purposeful* thought structure.

So go ahead now. Revisit your schedule or daily planner and dedicate just 15 minutes, if you haven't already, to doing nothing.

Remember, the commitment is to follow through with this schedule; having a no matter what attitude and removing the aspects of your usual day that have little or no support for the end objective.

It may seem highly regimented, but the more you build upon this foundation, the more *flexibility* you will find as you consciously remove aspects that have been draining your time/progress journey.

If you were to halve your time on social media, what shifts could you make to your daily schedule?

High Demanding Attitude

WHY NOW?

Benjamin Bonetti

MY SCRUFFY HAIR

How important is it really? For years in my coaching practice, I took the belief that in order to be the best, I had to present myself in a way that created a character, an *expectation* of the outside world.

This character and how well it was presented would determine my own success. I was wrong. From the type of shirt I wear, the chinos, the cut of the suit or even the registration/year of my car is not a representation of my *ability* to achieve or deliver.

In fact, the smokescreen that many put up is to distract the truth and the ability behind the message. And I mention this now because as you evolve, it's likely that your look beyond the materialistic may perhaps even relinquish some of those aspects that you didn't think were essential, or even attached to your *success*.

And simplify various other aspects of your life.

I'm unshaven, I don't use hair products because I don't like the chemicals used – and I turn up for interviews in shorts and flip-flops, not because I have little respect for anybody else but because it's where I feel most comfortable – and where I am able to *deliver* the best.

Sure I enjoy driving a nice car, I enjoy a tailor-made to suit, but it's not my identity, it certainly isn't a representation of truth or my ability as a professional coach.

And I mention this again because as you challenge your past beliefs, there will be aspects of your past life that will still matter and I'm okay with this. The question is not whether you enjoy the finer things in life but whether it's a smokescreen to avoid the realisation of *truth*.

It's not an area that I want to get caught up on and of course people have their own opinions, especially when people remove that judgement aspect of self – but just file this into the back of the mind somewhere – for a time where perhaps you ask yourself 'for what purpose'.

For what purpose am I using/buying/believing this is important to me – and why???

🎯 What smokescreens have you been putting up?

_____

_____

_____

_____

_____

_____

🎯 What security did this offer?

_____

_____

🎯 How can you shift this thinking?

_____
_____
_____
_____
_____
_____

🎯 How would this be more supportive to the future you?

_____
_____
_____
_____
_____
_____
_____
_____
_____
_____

HOW DOES IT LO- OK?

THE DESERT ISLAND

In this exercise, you're going to need a stopwatch and a pen.

This is a great exercise to repeat over the coming weeks and then compare how the results differ. There are no right or wrong answers within this exercise. It's entirely *dependent* on your current state.

> 🎯 Right now in the present moment, I'd like you to think about the past, having just three minutes to decide what you'd like to carry from the past through into the future. You have three minutes on your stopwatch. GO.
>
> _____
>
> _____
>
> _____
>
> _____
>
> _____
>
> _____

Stop

> 🎯 Follow the same process but go into the future. Go in to the future and decide what in the future you'd like to bring back to the present moment.
>
> _____
> _____
> _____
> _____
> _____

Stop

> 🎯 Now imagine yourself arriving onto the island with all that you have brought into the present from the past and all that you've brought into the present from the future.
>
> _____
> _____
> _____
> _____
> _____
> _____
> _____

🎯 Ask yourself right now if there is any aspects that you would change and why these changes would be made.

_____

_____

_____

_____

_____

_____

_____

_____

_____

_____

This exercise is a great way just to recheck whether you're *attracting* the right things into your life, when your mindset is focused on a future version of self, and a quick reminder that you will without conscious effort still reflect back to the past – and that's okay, it's where you are reflecting which is key.

Go through this list of 'things', remembering there is no right or wrong answers, just your answers, and see if there is anything that you're taking with you that is done so for anyone else?

WHAT NEXT?

PERSON AND CHARACTER

I have already explained the difference between personality and characters, with personality being the person that you are when pressure is applied, and the characters are the many people that you play on a daily basis depending on the circumstances in which you're placed.

[I'm not the person I am when working with a client that I would be when dealing with my children – if however, I am challenged by putting myself in a position where my flight, fight or freeze state is applied, then my personality will be shown.]

I mention this again because as we've covered in relationships, it is essential that we dig deep into *the true meaning* of who we are.

And that's okay...

and the purpose of challenging who you've become.

So right now, imagine yourself in the situation where you're completely alone, where it's a matter of life or death, where you cannot play a character to get yourself out of the situation.

The true version of you will come to fruition.

🎯 Who is this person?

_____
_____
_____
_____

🎯 If you could have a superpower at this moment, what would it be?

_____
_____
_____
_____
_____

🎯 Bringing this into reality, how can you have this or an adaptation?

_____
_____
_____

What benefits would this bring?

_____

_____

_____

_____

_____

_____

_____

What's stopping you from having this?

_____

_____

_____

_____

_____

_____

_____

HOW ARE YOU DEFINED?

ARE YOU SELFISH?

🎯 If you follow your own dreams and aspirations and it doesn't fall into another's wavelength, are you being selfish and why?

_____

_____

_____

_____

_____

This is something that comes up in almost every client one-to-one, how they were called selfish by childhood friends, parents and even loved ones.

In my world, this needs management, because on most occasions, it's not the individual that's being selfish, it's the *realisation* of another's own world which is in question.

As a result of that reflection, it can be deemed by another to seem selfish. Now, how quickly you can resolve this circumstance will depend on how stable and *solid* the relationship is, and how your communication has evolved.

My invitation to you is to be resilient in your journey, and avoid the temptation to play down your own *dreams* and aspirations to fit in with another person's ideal of the world.

Your life is your choice, and it's you that's going to have to live either with *fulfilment* or without. I remember an awkward conversation many years ago when a childhood friend of 20 years said that he couldn't be my friend anymore because my success was showing him up with his family and girlfriend.

It seems shocking when you put it down on paper but this is a very real conversation that many people have in their head but few *have the audacity* to say out loud.

People often do not reflect their behaviour. In fact, just as you have learnt at times, there can be more happening behind the scenes than meets the eye – with the temptation to conclude a perception of another you're closing any opportunities that may arise in the future.

Some of my closest friends perhaps would not be my friends if I would have taken their initial face value in the communication. I said before, remove the drama, but it's important to understand to leave the doors open so that should the individual evolve back into that space, there's an *opportunity* for them to bring the relationship back up to a level which you choose that is acceptable.

> How have you been restricted in the past as a result of feeling selfish?
>
> _____
>
> _____

🎯 How would things have turned out differently if you had acted in your best interest?

WHAT IS BIGGER FOR YOU?

WHAT IS THE INTENTION OF THIS THOUGHT?

If you questioned the intention of every thought that you had, how much more productive would *you* be?

It's important to be realistic in our expectations of the availability to achieve, but I'm going to invite you to *question the intentions* of all of your actions, your behaviours, relationships and internal communication.

As you increase the level of control that you take and slow down the processes, perhaps you would choose to change some unproductive behaviours that you demonstrated in the past or even how you enter into a space.

The intention as you enter into an internal dialog radically changes the conversations that are produced and the *answers* that are provided.

TALKING AS THE FIRST PERSON IN THE THIRD PERSON

Many exercises that you use in training the mind include talking as the third person, you may find that you've been talking about your third person being completely disassociated with the ownership of self.

My recommendation here, and it's part of the improvement in

language, would be to remove any dissociation when describing self.

This may cause conflict amongst my peers, but what I have found in coaching some of the elite is that by adding *ownership* and visualising events through your own eyes, creates the pathways internally and the familiarity required to deliver.

It removes the 'what did they do?' and shifts it to 'how did I do it?'

The shift in language and ownership has proven time and time again to create *fantastic results* in times of increased stress.

I invite you to adopt this shift in thinking if you haven't already, especially when utilising visualisation to guide you and control self.

What Is The Intention Of This Thought

THE INTE- NT- ION?

NATURE VERSUS NURTURE

This a tricky one and is an area where there are masses of studies to argue for and against. The one thing for sure is both have a place – both have *significant evidence* to support their claims – and both have an important role to play when it comes to elite athletes.

There's no getting away from our genetic makeup, the environmental factors during our adolescence – and the nurture from parents, coaches and anyone else who has supported inspiring athletes during their younger days.

But even those who don't have the genetic makeup similar to those performing at the elite level should not be discouraged. There's very real reason why.

A large majority of those with *natural* DNA have the perfect genome to support that discipline but do not have the *mindset* or determination to deliver.

A five foot, two basketball player is unlikely to reach the same potential as those at six foot five to seven feet, but those at six foot three with the drive and *determination* still have in my opinion an equal opportunity.

This hardware vs. software debate will go on into the future and is not an area that I want to focus the efforts on now, but I'm sure that if you're at this stage and *looking* to improve your mental performance, you've developed to a certain level which is beyond the 'basics' of sport selection.

If you're not at this stage, then I beg you right now to separate yourself from the fact/fiction thought process. I invite you to do this, not because I'm looking to belittle any dreams or aspirations, but for those 1%ers, having the body to build upon is certainly a *foundation* that can't be missed.

[I will unlikely ever be able to be a sprinter, not because I can't sprint but my slow and fast twitch fibres are not in the correct coloration compared to those at the upper performers. With training I can improve, but certain bone growth factors further inhibit my natural ability to progress beyond a threshold not forgetting my age and the investment required to get to this place.]

HONESTY PLEASE…

> 🎯 Can you improve based on any physical limitations?
> _____
> _____
> _____
> _____
> _____
> _____
> _____

Nature Versus Nurture

CAN YOU OWN THIS?

Benjamin Bonetti

PRACTICE ON YOUR OWN

This concept has aggravated some of the sporting teams that I've worked with over the last few years, not because I've taken anything away from them but because the 'traditional' coaching method is to *work* within the team at every awakening hour.

For me, a minimum of three hours per week practising alone has proven to be worth the short-term shift and reduce the 'choking' effect that some team players experience when entering a structured team training session.

I've seen some of the most *promising* athletes fail within weeks of entering team environments, not because of the inability to work within the team but because they have lacked the 'breathing space' that allowed them to reach this place in the first instance.

From newly promoted premier football players to equestrians, the effects can be disastrous unless addressed early on.

> 🎯 What would you do if you could incorporate just three hours training on your own?
>
> _____
>
> _____
>
> _____

So that's it – I've come to the conclusion of this "Introduction Into Building Mental Toughness". I'm sure there will be more thinking that is spurred, and I hope that you join me by downloading my audiobook *"The New Encyclopaedia Of Sports Psychology"*, or if not, you can head over to Amazon and pick up a copy packed full of the strategies and techniques that have helped clients from keen amateurs to Olympic medallists.

It's a small price to pay for such fundamental results.

MOST WON'T TAKE ACTION

MY QUESTION FOR YOU ISNT WHETHER YOU WILL OR WILL NOT...

BUT ARE YOU READY?

50%
DISCOUNT FOR THOSE ACTION TAKERS

ENTER: commit50 AT CHECKOUT:

http://100nman.com/7-day-athlete-mindset-shift/

Printed in the USA
CPSIA information can be obtained
at www.ICGtesting.com
LVHW011334311023
762540LV00002B/122